THE HISTORY AND TECHNIQUES
OF THE GREAT MASTERS

REMBRANDT

THE HISTORY AND TECHNIQUES OF THE GREAT MASTERS

REMBRANDT

Andrew Morrall

CHARTWELL
BOOKS, INC.

A QUARTO BOOK

Published by Chartwell Books
A Division of Book Sales, Inc.
110 Enterprise Avenue
Secaucus, New Jersey 07094

ISBN 1-55521-211-5

This book was designed and produced by
Quarto Publishing plc
The Old Brewery, 6 Blundell Street
London N7 9BH

Senior Editor Polly Powell
Art Editor Vincent Murphy

Project Editor Hazel Harrison
Designer Terry Smith
Picture Researcher Celestine Dars

Art Director Moira Clinch
Editorial Director Carolyn King

Many thanks to Bob Cocker and Paul Swain

Typeset by QV Typesetting Ltd

Manufactured in Hong Kong by Regent
Publishing Services Limited
Printed in Hong Kong by Leefung-Asco
Printers Ltd

CONTENTS

INTRODUCTION

REMBRANDT
Self-portrait
1640
National Gallery, London

Rembrandt van Rijn was undoubtedly the greatest interpreter of the human personality in the history of painting. Throughout a long and very productive career his two overriding interests were portraiture and Biblical narrative subjects. In the human face, and not least his own — over sixty self-portraits by him still exist — he could "study" character, personality and temperament, while the Bible provided him with a limitless range of subjects through which to explore powerful human emotions. Rembrandt saw the Bible stories as products of human experience, and more than any other painter, he interpreted them in bold, unidealized human terms. Equally his vision of human nature was colored to a considerable degree by his reading of the Bible; many of his portraits read almost as meditations, often seeming to carry the same sense of moral weight as his paintings of the Old Testament prophets. To these powerful depictions of human nature he brought a highly original technique which pushed the possibilities of the oil-painting medium to extraordinary limits. In terms of technique Rembrandt remains the greatest individualist of the seventeenth century, and the natural heir to Titian (c1487-1576), his great sixteenth-century forebear.

The content of his paintings cannot be separated from his style. His highly allusive commentaries on human life, time, age and experience demanded experiments in the medium that took him far beyond the limited vocabulary of contemporary practice. And as his attitude to his subject matter deepened over time, so his technique became increasingly personal, to the point at which, in his last years, he completely stepped outside the stylistic conventions of his day.

The young Rembrandt

Rembrandt was born in Leyden on July 15, 1606, at the start of what was to be for Holland an unprecedented period of peace and prosperity. Three years earlier, the Twelve Year Truce with Spain had been signed, which in effect signified Spain's recognition of the independence of the Dutch Republic and the end of a long and burdensome war. Rembrandt was thus born into a relatively young and optimistic culture, made resolute through its successful opposition to a larger power, economically vital, and relatively liberal in its political and religious practice. He was the son of a miller, Harman van Rijn — the family name derives from the mill that stood on the banks of the Old Rhine just outside Leyden — and was the eighth of nine children, only four of whom were to survive to maturity. Although in later life Rembrandt was to marry into the wealthy patrician class of Amsterdam and fully participate in the cultured, artistic world of the capital, he maintained throughout his life a brusqueness of manner and an impatience with social niceties that betrayed his modest origins. Filippo Baldinucci, writing in 1686, complained that the "ugly and plebeian face by which he was ill-favored, was accompanied by untidy and dirty clothes, since it was his custom, when working, to wipe his brushes on himself, and to do other things of a similar nature."

At the age of fourteen he was enrolled at the University of Leyden, a relatively unusual step for one of his class, and perhaps an indication that he was considered exceptionally bright. His inclination toward painting, however, must already have been strong, for after only a few months he left and became apprenticed to a local painter, Jacob van Swanenburgh, who specialized in both portraits and depictions of hell in the tradition of Hieronymus Bosch (c1450-1516). No trace of this artist's influence can be found in Rembrandt's subsequent work.

It was not until 1624 that Rembrandt, doubtless impatient with the provincial nature of Leyden's artistic circles, spent six months in the studio of the fashionable Amsterdam artist, Peter Lastman, and first came into contact with an artistic personality of real stature.

Lastman had been trained by the leading Flemish Mannerist artist, Cornelis Cornelisz van Haarlem, and had lived for some time in Rome, where he became familiar with the art of Adam Elsheimer (1578-1610) and the leading southern Baroque painters. He specialized in Biblical and mythological subjects, and his style, which combined the polished paint surfaces and stylized classicism of Flemish Mannerism with a vigorous and realistic attitude to his subject matter, left a deep impression on the young artist. Rembrandt's interest in Biblical subjects and realistic portrayal, as well as his taste for exotic and romantic settings and costume details both seem to have been stimulated by his contact with Lastman, and the paintings he executed on his return to Leyden reflect this debt. Works like *Anna Accused by Tobit of Stealing the Kid* (see page 17) display an almost over-emphatic realism, a desire for the exact delineation of expression and gesture to convey emotion, very close to the manner of Lastman.

The technique of chiaroscuro

The other major influence on Rembrandt's emerging style was that of the Utrecht School, the Dutch followers of the Italian artist, Caravaggio. Working principally in Rome and Naples at the beginning of the century, Michelangelo Caravaggio (1573-1610) had created a strikingly original style of painting that combined a vigorous "peasant" realism with violent contrasts of light and shade which conveyed an impression of intense drama. This technique, called chiaroscuro (literally "light-dark"), was adopted by artists all over Europe and became a major stylistic feature of seventeenth-century painting. The Utrecht "Caravaggisti" adopted the same deep tenebroso effects, but tended to use them for less violent subjects than Caravaggio himself. Gerrit van Honthorst's *Christ before the High Priest* shows this style very clearly, and also illustrates the common device of introducing some kind of light, often a burning taper, into the composition as the primary light-source.

Rembrandt adopted this chiaroscuro technique early in his career, and for the rest of his life it was to be the main expressive vehicle of his work. He recognized in this shadowy light — in the deep well of a darkened interior or in a flickering murk of half-tones and reflections — the power of suggestion, of metaphor, the ability to create mood and to suggest realms of thought and feeling beyond the concrete surfaces of the material world. By cloaking his figures in a veil of shadows and half-lights, he created a shift of attention from the tangible world of perceived objects to the intangible one of spirit and feeling.

REMBRANDT
Self-portrait
c 1629, National Gallery,
London

The deep shadow covering the face is an early and crudely forceful example of the device

Rembrandt developed of using light and shadow to heighten the psychological suggestiveness of the image. Here the spectator is forced to complete the sitter's features in the imagination.

Clearly his painting technique was determined by his chosen style, and he early on adopted a method of painting from dark to light, beginning to work with a uniform underlayer of a fairly dark brown and building up the major forms in increasingly lighter tones, finishing with the highlights. (Generally in Rembrandt's work the thinnest areas of paint are found in the darkest areas and the thickest in the highlights.)

A boldly experimental approach can already be seen in the early *Self-portrait* painted about 1629. The shadow falls over the face so as to virtually conceal the expression, something no other artist had hitherto attempted. He is also experimenting with different effects of texture. There are expressive differences between the rough impasto of the collar and the thinner painting of the jerkin. The background has been achieved by dragging a brush loaded heavily with fairly dry paint over a darker background, allowing the darks to show through the pitted troughs left by the brush hairs and thus creating a sense of surface shimmer. The wild, unkempt curls of the hair have been created in part by using a blunt instrument, possibly the wooden end of his paintbrush, literally to carve the lines through the upper layer of paint and reveal the underlayer beneath.

Such a rough, vigorous treatment, such a deliberate lack of "finish," complements the unadorned and uncompromising realism of the portrait. Rembrandt seems at this point to be deliberately exaggerating his coarse, disheveled nature. The immediate impression created is of an extremely forceful individual and romantic temperament, and one that was attempting to flout the existing standards of portraiture. The serious, questioning expression, half-hidden in deep shadow, seems to have more in common with the nineteenth-century Romantic vision than with the urbane polish of fashionable seventeenth-century practice.

PETER LASTMAN
*Juno Discovering Jupiter
with Io*
1618, National Gallery, London

Juno, on the left, descends to earth with crown, scepter and peacocks, and discovers her husband Jupiter with the nymph Io, whom he hastily turns into a heifer. Winged Cupid and Deceit, in mask and foxskin, casts a drapery over her. The classical subject and Italianate handling typify Lastman's mature style.

Success and prosperity

The originality of Rembrandt's art was evidently soon noticed, for by at least 1629 he had met Constantijn Huygens, secretary to the Prince of Orange. Huygens was a man who had traveled widely in his capacity as civil servant and diplomat, and was possessed of wide cultural interests, his great passion being painting. He was immediately struck by the work of this young miller's son and by that of another fellow Leyden painter, Jan Lievens; in his autobiography he stated that they already equaled the famous masters and would soon surpass them. It was almost certainly through the encouragement and connections of this man that Rembrandt was induced to move to Amsterdam in 1631, and there he embarked on the happiest and most successful period of his life. He quickly established his reputation as a skilled and accomplished portrait painter with *The Anatomy Lesson of Dr Tulp*, his first large-scale group commission, and thereafter he was in constant demand for portraits. For his commissioned works of this period he adopted the polished and elegant realism that characterized the style of other leading portraitists of the day, such as Willem de Keyser, holding back the freedom of technique he had developed at Leyden.

In 1634 Rembrandt married his landlord's first cousin, Saskia van Ulenborch. Saskia's family were of the professional class of Amsterdam, and she brought him a sizeable dowry as well as connections in wealthy patrician circles. Their marriage, though tragically short-lived, appears to have been extremely happy, and Saskia's pale, coquettish features appear repeatedly in paintings, etchings and drawings throughout the 1630s.

Rembrandt was now successful, popular and prosperous. By 1639 he and Saskia had bought themselves a large house in the Joden-Breestraat, and Rembrandt had begun to amass a large collection of paintings, drawings and prints of old masters and contemporaries, as well as a varied collection of exotic curios. What evidence there is suggests that the young couple lived a fashionable and extravagant lifestyle, and in Rembrandt's art at this time one also senses the same exuberance and self-indulgence. This is perhaps best seen in the extraordinary double portrait of himself and Saskia that must date from the mid-1630s. It shows the artist, extravagantly dressed, raising his glass with a wide, almost leering smile on his face, and with a much more sedate Saskia on his knee. While it is unlikely that this work was intended as a straight representation (the presence of a peacock, symbol of pride, possibly alludes to a scene from the life of the prodigal son), it shows the spirit with which Rembrandt was approaching his art and perhaps his life.

The work also shows the extent to which he was attempting to come to grips with the dynamic conception and rhetoric of the High Baroque style of the "Caravaggisti" and of Rubens, whose paintings Rembrandt was aware of through engravings. His other major paintings of the 1630s are no less extravagantly theatrical in both composition and conception. In *Belshazzar's Feast* (see page 25) he has taken over the Baroque device of catching a single moment of high drama and freezing his characters in split-second gestures of instantaneous reaction. The figures are pushed forward toward the picture plane within a cramped space, seeming as though about to burst the confines of the canvas. The effect is melodramatic and perhaps a little forced — instantaneity was not Rembrandt's chief forte.

Family tragedy and new directions

By the 1640s, as if aware that he had explored this theatricality to the full and recognized its limitations, he began to change his style in a process that continued throughout the next decade. He gradually dropped the violence, clamor and extravagance of gesture and adopted a tone of quieter, more restrained emotion. This

GERRIT VAN HONTHORST
Christ before the High Priest
c 1617, National Gallery, London

Honthorst was known as "Gherardo della notte," ("Gerard of the night") in Italy, where he lived from about 1610 to 1620, because of his interest in nocturnal or dimly lit scenes. He was important in transmitting the use of chiaroscuro from Italy to the Netherlands, and thus was an influence on Rembrandt.

change in his art is usually attributed to the tragic events of his personal life. Three children born to Saskia died in early infancy — only the fourth, Titus, was to live to early adulthood — and Saskia too was ailing, perhaps as a result of child-bearing. Numerous drawings and etchings show her sinking slowly from glowing health to a sickly, bed-ridden state. She died in June, 1642.

From this point onward Rembrandt was to be increasingly burdened by financial worries and a waning in popularity. The 1640s saw the rise in Amsterdam of a taste for the elegant, courtly portraiture of artists like van Dyck, a style for which Rembrandt had little sympathy and to which he refused to adapt. Commissions accordingly went in increasing numbers to his more flexible pupils, but his decline in popularity was by no means as dramatic as is often believed. His greatest

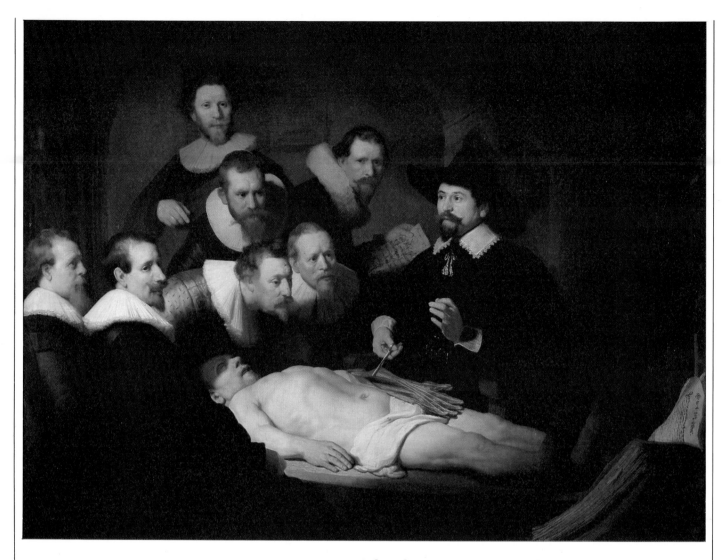

REMBRANDT
*The Anatomy Lesson of
Dr Tulp*
1632, Mauritshuis, The Hague

In this early masterpiece
Rembrandt solved the problem
of group portraiture, namely

how to reconcile interest,
variety and compositional
unity with faithful and
suitably dignified likenesses.
Attention has been focused on
the corpse, with the onlookers
arranged around it in varying
attitudes of concentration.

showpiece of group-portraiture, the celebrated *Night Watch* of 1642 (see page 33) was very highly regarded even by his more classically minded critics, and he maintained a steady, if reduced, flow of commissions. His gradual rejection of fashionable taste should perhaps be regarded as a symptom of his deepening awareness of himself as an artist and of the nature and direction of his art. This new awareness is clear in the *Self-portrait* of 1640 (see page 29), in which he shows himself dressed expensively, as was appropriate to a successful painter, but in a mood that is sharply serious and quite at odds with the showy flamboyance of earlier self-portraits.

The new element of restraint signals a profound change in Rembrandt's artistic outlook, which partly found expression in an awakened sense of nature, witnessed by the many landscape drawings and etchings that he carried out in these years. Done with a wonderful economy of line, they show a very direct response to the fields and copses outside the city, together with a feeling for space and rolling skies quite unlike that of his earlier, less realistic and more romantic treatments.

The same directness can also be discerned in his handling of human subjects. He abandoned the theatricality of his earlier style and began to choose calmer, more serene subjects, especially those from the life of Christ, which allowed him to explore more generalized and more enduring human qualities. One senses a closing in of his social life, a reluctance to look beyond his family and immediate circle for inspiration. In a number of sketches and drawings that date from this period, such as the *Two Women Teaching a Child to Walk* one recognizes the same sense of domestic tenderness that can also be found in many small-scale works of the childhood of Christ, for instance the *Adoration of the Shepherds* (see page 39). His style in both drawing and painting shows an increasing impatience with descrip-

REMBRANDT'S PAINTING METHODS

In Rembrandt's paintings the paint was always thinnest in the background, and here the color of the brown priming can be seen through the top layer.

In parts of Belshazzar's Feast *the paint is built up thickly and then partially carved away with a sharp instrument.*

Rembrandt often used thin, transparent glazes over thick impastos, as in this detail of Woman Bathing.

In Rembrandt's day and before it, painting was a far slower and more laborious business than it is today, when paintings are often completed in one or two sessions. Advances in the manufacture of artist's materials have given us the boon of ready-primed canvases, pre-mixed, permanent colors and fast-drying mediums, but in the seventeenth century canvases had to be measured, stretched and primed, and pigments ground, mixed and stored before the real work could begin. Sometimes many of these preliminaries were done by artists' apprentices or studio hands, but a painting still had to be built up layer by layer, often with a long drying time between each one.

Rembrandt worked on a medium-brown ground consisting of ocher bound with resin and animal glue, a method introduced by Titian and used more or less universally until the nineteenth century, when white or light-toned grounds began to be favored by artists such as the French Impressionists. He has left no sketches or preliminary studies; his compositions were mapped out directly onto the canvas in a monochrome underpainting, producing what is known as a "dead-color painting" ready to be worked up. Over this he applied his body color, working from background to foreground, leaving the figures at the front as monochrome silhouettes until their turn came.

His palette was small even by seventeenth-century standards, but he was a superlative colorist, managing to retain a balance between color itself and tonality — the use of light and shade.

The range of colors Rembrandt used was quite small by modern standards. Those illustrated here, with the addition of lead white, were the ones used in Belshazzar's Feast.

1 Black; 2 Brown (precise pigment not known); 3 Red ocher; 4 Transparent browns, probably Cologne earth and bistre; 5 Vermilion and organic red lakes; 6 Lead tin yellow, usually mixed with lead white; 7 Azurite; 8 Smalt; 9 Greens, made by mixing lead tin yellow with azurite and smalt

tive details and a desire to capture the expressive essence of an attitude or gesture with the greatest economy.

Part of this new harmony in Rembrandt's art was possibly due to the presence in his household of Hendrickje Stoffels, a peasant girl who in about 1645 had been taken on as a nurse for Titus, supplanting another woman, one Geertge Dix, both in her capacity as surrogate mother and in her employer's affections. (Geertge won an extremely bitter legal battle claiming unfair dismissal, but Rembrandt retaliated in a revealing display of obduracy, and managed to have her locked up in a house of correction in Gouda.) Thereafter Hendrickje became in effect his common-law wife, looking after his needs and eventually bearing him a daughter. They never married, possibly because Rembrandt would thereby have forfeited the small allowance left to him under the terms of Saskia's will. Hendrickje was the complete opposite of Saskia, yet it is clear from the many paintings and drawings in which she appears that she and Rembrandt settled down into a life of domestic contentment.

REMBRANDT
Self-portrait with Saskia
c1635, Staatliche
Kunstammlungen, Dresden

One of the strangest of all Rembrandt's self-portraits, this

was probably intended more as a general genre or narrative scene in the manner of the Dutch "Caravaggisti" than as a specific double portrait, though a personal level of meaning cannot be ruled out.

REMBRANDT
Two Women Teaching a Child to Walk
Pen and ink

In a few rapid strokes Rembrandt manages to convey

a precise idea of personality in each figure, as well as a sense of the rapt absorption of the two women (perhaps mother and grandmother) in the child as it takes its first tentative steps.

The later years

The last twenty years of Rembrandt's life were nonetheless dogged by financial hardship and personal tragedy. Partly due to his natural acquisitiveness and extravagance, partly to the ever-dwindling income from commissions, and partly also to the generally worsening state of the Dutch economy, debts began to accumulate around his large house on the Breestraat. In 1656, in order to ensure an inheritance for Titus, he placed the house in his son's name and borrowed more in order to purchase another, smaller house. But a short time later he was forced to declare himself insolvent and to pledge all his belongings to pay off his debts. The liquidization of his property was ordered and an inventory of his goods drawn up and placed on public auction. This inventory still exists, providing an interesting insight into his tastes and collecting habits. It shows him to have been an extremely eclectic collector of works of art, listing paintings not only by contemporary masters such as Hercules Seghers, Jan Lievens and Porcellis, but also works attributed to such great names as Giorgione, Palma Vecchio and Raphael. In addition, there were literally thousands of prints and drawings, ranging from Renaissance masters to Persian miniatures. Other objects included a large collection of arms and armor, oriental costumes and bowls, and a miscellany of natural objects such as shells and stuffed birds.

Above
REMBRANDT
View across the Nieuwe Meer near Amsterdam
Pen and brush, brown ink, on colored ground

In the 1640s, during long walks, Rembrandt recorded the countryside around Amsterdam in a series of drawings and etchings. Here he marvelously suggests the action of a light wind across its sluggish surface.

Top
REMBRANDT
Landscape with Trees
Pen and ink

Executed not with a quill but with a reed pen, which gives broad strokes and a softening effect, this drawing, with its rapid and rhythmical strokes, contrasts with the more deliberate and calculated use of tinted paper and broad, translucent washes of the later work illustrated above.

of contemporary art to develop so personal a manner of painting as to completely transcend all stylistic categories. Contemporaries often failed to understand his intentions, complaining that his works seemed unfinished, and Arnold Houbraken wrote in 1718 of a portrait by Rembrandt that "the colors were so heavily loaded that you could lift it from the floor by its nose." Certainly his manner became increasingly broad and his application of paint increasingly thick.

In the late portraits and self-portraits it is possible to discern a somber, rather pessimistic mood that may reflect the sad events of his personal life. Yet it was also in this period of his life that he could produce works of a depth and meaning unsurpassed in the whole history of art. In a work like *The Jewish Bride* (see page 59), one sees the distillation of pure feeling, expressed in terms of an awesome solemnity that fully conveys both the grandeur of the human spirit and the power of human love.

REMBRANDT
Saskia Lying in Bed
Ink drawing

This is one of a number of drawings of Saskia in bed that witness her gradual decline from health. Here, accompanied by a nurse at the foot of the bed, she looks decidedly depressed, her chin resting dejectedly on her hand.

The sale of his effects did very little to pay off his creditors, and in an attempt to keep him at least minimally solvent, Hendrickje and Titus formed a company which in effect employed Rembrandt and paid him a salary out of his own earnings, thus preventing his creditors from taking away any money he made. In this manner he continued to survive, albeit in a meager way, but tragedy was to strike him further. In 1663 Hendrickje died, followed five years later by Titus. Rembrandt struggled on briefly with his young daughter, but he too died the following year, alone and in obscurity.

Despite the hardship and adversity of his last years, this final period of his life witnessed an important development of his art and an extraordinary extension of his technique. In his old age, indifferent to fashion and worldly opinion, he was free to abandon the conventions

CHRONOLOGY OF REMBRANDT'S LIFE

1606	July 15th: Rembrandt born in Leyden.
1613-20	Attends the Latin School in Leyden.
1620	Enrolled at the University of Leyden.
1621-23	Apprenticed to the painter Jacob van Swanenburgh.
1624	Spends about six months in the studio of Peter Lastman in Amsterdam.
1626	Established as independent artist in Leyden. Paints *Tobit and Anna*.
1630	Favorably noticed by Constantijn Huygens. Paints *Jeremiah Lamenting the Destruction of Jerusalem*.
1631	Moves to Amsterdam.
1632	Establishes reputation with *The Anatomy Lesson of Dr Tulp*.
1634	July 22nd: marries Saskia van Ulenborch.
1635	December 1st: Saskia gives birth to Rumbartus, who dies shortly afterwards. *Belshazzar's Feast* painted around this time.
1638	July: birth of daughter, Cornelia, who dies within a month.
1639	Rembrandt and Saskia move into large house on the Jodenbreestraat.
1640	July: birth of second daughter, Cornelia, who also does not survive. Paints *Self-portrait*.
1641	July: birth of son, Titus, the only one of their children to reach maturity.
1642	June 5th: Saskia dies. Geertje Dix employed as nurse for Titus. Completes *The Night Watch*.
1646	Paints the *Adoration of the Shepherds*, perhaps to a

Anna Accused by Tobit of Stealing the Kid

Adoration of the Shepherds

Young Woman Bathing

	commission from the Stadtholder, Frederick Henry.
1648	Geertje Dix leaves Rembrandt's service and brings case against him for unfair dismissal. By this time Hendrickje Stoffels has entered Rembrandt's employ.
1654	Rembrandt and Hendrickje summoned before the Ecclesiastical Court, accused of concubinage.
1654	Hendrickje gives birth to a daughter, Cornelia.
1655	Paints *Young Woman Bathing*.
1656	To avoid bankrupcy, Rembrandt applies to the High Court for a "cessio bonorum," and declares himself insolvent. Liquidaton of his property ordered and inventory of his belongings made.
1657-8	Rembrandt's goods disposed of by public auction.
1660	Moves into smaller house in the more modest Rozengracht. Hendrickje and Titus form a company that "employs" Rembrandt, and receives all his work, in return for a salary, in order to keep the creditors at bay. Paints *The Denial of St Peter*.
1661	Painted the *Portrait of Margaretha de Geer*.
1663	July 21st: Hendrickje dies. *Self-Portrait with Maulstick, Palette and Brushes* painted about this time.
1664-68	The *Jewish Bride* painted about this time.
1668	September 4th: Titus dies.
1669	October 4th: Rembrandt dies. Four days afterward he is buried in the Westerkerk, beside Hendrickje and Titus.

THE PAINTINGS

ANNA ACCUSED BY TOBIT OF STEALING THE KID

1626
15½ × 11¾ in / 39.5 × 30 cm
Oil on panel
Rijsmuseum, Amsterdam

This small-scale panel is one of Rembrandt's earliest independent works, executed shortly after the months spent in Peter Lastman's studio. It shows both his debt to the older painter and the measure of his independence. Lastman's influence is seen in the vividly observed expressions of the blind couple (traditionally believed to be Rembrandt's parents) as well as in the minutely accurate brushwork. The chiaroscuro — the dividing of the composition into areas of strong light and shade — is tentative, serving merely to bring out the characters in strong relief, and possessing none of the expressive power of his later works.

Yet the roots of his mature style are apparent here. Already he is working from dark colors to light, beginning his composition by applying a layer of dark brown to the whole surface and building up the forms by successive applications of lighter paint. The thinnest areas of paint are thus the darkest, indeed the vertical grain of the wood panel can be distinguished in the deep shadow between the two figures. The dark underpainting serves as the chief unifying tone, occurring not only in the background but also in areas such as the kid's hind leg and in the shadows of Anna's skirt and neck.

These darkest areas are then modified by layers of lighter colors, which define the forms of the painting. The paving stones on the floor by Tobit's feet, for instance, are made up of a lighter, greenish gray, leaving lines of the darker underlayer showing through as the divisions between them. (Rembrandt has actually carved his initials and the date into the wet upper layer of paint, probably with the wooden end of his paintbrush, revealing the darker paint beneath.) By contrast, the shadows cast by the old man's stick are painted in a dark brown layer, applied over the color of the paving stones. Another vivid example of overlapping paint layers can be seen in the hindquarters of the young goat,

where the greenish gray of the wall is clearly painted over the dark brown underpaint of the tail. To indicate the fur, Rembrandt has applied a rough and very thin layer of brown paint over the green-gray of the wall, allowing it to show through, and has suggested individual hairs by, again, carving with a blunt instrument into the wet paint.

Looked at closely, it becomes apparent that the initial impression of high finish is deceptive. Already, even when working on so small a scale, he is loading his brush with more paint than is strictly necessary, and the wrinkled hands and face of the old man reveal a completely original method of using thick paint to almost model the forms in high relief. The wrinkles of the brow have been individually drawn, the brushstrokes following precisely the forms they describe, but in paint so thick that they actually stand out in relief from the darker layer beneath. A single uneven brushstroke is made not only to describe the form of the wrinkle, but also the texture of the weathered skin. Where the skin is still firm, such as along the ridge of the nose, a much thinner, smoother brushstroke has been used. The same method of capturing the texture of objects through imitative brushwork can again be found in the fur of Tobit's sleeve, where tiny, overlapping strokes have been brushed over the darker ground in a fluid, wet-into-wet technique. Rembrandt's thumbprint is visible in the patch of yellow beneath the elbow, where he has lightly touched the wet paint to blend the tones.

It is striking to compare this painstaking method of exact representation of form in low relief with the mature Rembrandt's broad suggestion of form by means of thick impasto. At this stage of his development he creates an almost perfect illusion of reality through attention to minute surface detail. Only the slightly looser modeling of the walking stick on the lower left breaks the spell.

The minute handling, precise description and intimate scale of this work are typical of Rembrandt's "Leyden period" of the 1620s. Indeed, through the influence of one of his earliest pupils, Gerrit Dou, this painstaking realism became the characteristic of a subsequent generation of Leyden painters, known as the "Leyden *fijnschilder*," or "fine painters." The style remained extremely popular there long after Rembrandt had left for Amsterdam and learnt to broaden his style. No other contemporary Leyden painter, however, could equal Rembrandt's depiction of character and human emotion, as in this scene where Tobit berates his wife for having — as he mistakenly believes — stolen a kid to alleviate their poverty.

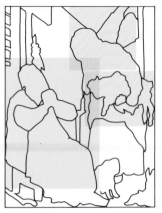

1

2

1 The details of the background wall behind Anna's head have been sketched in lightly with a dull earth-green over a darker ground. The basket is an example of literal description, of meticulous drawing in color — and in relief.

2 The building up of forms from dark to light is well illustrated here, from the "base" of dark brown of the hind leg to the lighter strokes of fur and the powerful modeling of Anna's gnarled hands. The greenish gray of the wall can be seen to overlap the dark of the hind leg. A very thin glaze of brown has been laid over the green-gray at the extremities of the fur, and scraped through in curling strokes to suggest individual hairs.

3 *Actual size detail* The head of Tobit is a marvelous example of descriptive modeling in three dimensions. A separate brushstroke describes each wrinkle of the forehead, following its exact shape and volume. A loaded brush has been dragged unevenly across the dome, leaving a broken surface that conveys the impression of ageing skin and contrasts expressively with the extremely fine strokes that make up the individual hairs of the beard.

The range of technique employed is also evident in the clothing. On the bottom edge of Tobit's sleeve minute touches of varying shape, density and color have been stroked over each other.

3 *Actual size detail*

JEREMIAH LAMENTING THE DESTRUCTION OF JERUSALEM

Signed and dated 1630
22¾×18in/58×46cm
Oil on panel
Rijksmuseum, Amsterdam

In this small jewel-like painting, executed four years after the previous example, a marked broadening of technique is evident, as well as a deepening of the artist's sense of color and a fuller understanding of the expressive uses of chiaroscuro. The aged prophet sits sunk in an introspective gloom below a dimly perceived pillar. To the left, the ruined city is in flames, above which, traced in very fluid paint, the Angel of the Lord can be seen, bringing down death and destruction as the prophet had foretold.

Throughout his life Rembrandt was fascinated by the portrayal of old age. He evidently used his parents as models at the start of his career, as the same elderly faces occur repeatedly in a series of early works. They, of course, provided him with free models whose features and characters he knew well, yet on a deeper level the whole theme of old age held a strong sway over his imagination and he turned to it repeatedly, portraying it in terms of the summation of a life's experience rather than as infirmity or senility. He was particularly attracted to the aged seers and prophets of the Bible, figures of great wisdom and moral stature; and his renderings of the deeply etched lines of a forehead or an absorbed and introspective stare, demonstrate a sympathy and an understanding that has more to do with an attitude to life itself than with the interpretation of any single individual. His aged figures seem to express a vision of profound human goodness, born of knowledge and experience.

It is the chiaroscuro that sets the emotional key of this painting. The deep shadows which encroach from above and from the side of the prophet contribute powerfully to his mood of hopeless despair. Once again Rembrandt has built up his composition from a dark background by using successive layers of lighter tones. The brushwork is broader and no longer so doggedly descriptive, and the transition from the deepest shadow of the background to the lighter tones of the middle ground has been achieved by a layer of broadly painted, thin, tawny yellow, overlaid in turn by a thicker passage of greenish gray. The murky form of the huge pillar has been picked out in the same thin yellow together with touches of a light gray. These broad areas contrast with the rich, vigorous brushwork of the robe and the firm modeling of the foot. The glinting highlights of the embroidered gown and the golden vessels have been applied in minute touches of thick lead-white impasto, while the shadows have been given greater depth and luminosity by additional glazes of tinted brown. In both the embroidery work on the prophet's chest and the treatment of the bush on the left, Rembrandt's technique of scraping away the top layer of paint with a sharp instrument is again visible. By these means an extremely sophisticated tonal range is created which, together with a more expressive use of deep colors, shows his increasing mastery of his medium.

Rembrandt's artistic development can be gauged in the way he has moved away from the precise rendering of descriptive details in every part of the picture toward psychological and emotional emphasis by means of lighting, color contrasts and varied brushwork. Here he focuses attention on the prophet by placing him dramatically at the juncture of the light and shadow as well as by contrasting the detailed modeling, rich colors and thick impasto of the figure with surrounding passages of extreme thinness. This creates a sense of spatial depth also.

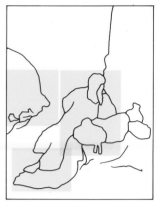

1

1 The ruins of Jerusalem, the flames and the huddled figures have been evoked with extreme economy, using four colors, each thinly laid over the other, in a fluid wet-on-wet technique. The green of the bush has been partially scraped away in rapid, scribbled strokes.

2 The prophet's foot has been modeled with great accuracy, and the subtle distribution of light and shade over the network of veins precisely recorded. Thin strokes of white follow the ridges of the folds of the gown, executed in minute hatchings, and the deepest areas of shadow are overlaid with glazes of deep black. The pale underlayer is plainly visible beneath the tawny crimson of the robe.

3 *Actual size detail* The bulbous forms of the golden bowl have been sketched in in dark brown outlines over a greenish-ocher middle ground, and the highlights filled in with tawny yellow. Thick drops of lead-white impasto, tinted with yellow, make up the points of reflected light. The technique of scratching through the top paint layer, used here to suggest embroidery on the prophet's chest, is clearly visible. The effect of the wrinkled skin on the arm has been suggested by an uneven, pitted surface of white impasto dragged across a darker underlayer. The deepest areas of shadow — beneath the Bible and on Jeremiah's left shoulder — have been created by the addition of dark brown, translucent glazes.

2

3 *Actual size detail*

BELSHAZZAR'S FEAST

Signed (with indistinct date) c 1637
66×82¼in/167.5×209cm
Oil on canvas
National Gallery, London

By the mid-1630s Rembrandt had established his reputation as a successful young painter in Amsterdam and set about coming to terms with the International High Baroque style. He was undoubtedly familiar with the work of Rubens and of monumental painting in Flanders and Italy, if only through engraved reproductions, and he now tried his hand at painting on a large scale himself, adopting all the stylistic "tricks" of the Baroque painters. Here he has chosen a story that allowed him to exploit to the full his love of exotic costumes and rich objects. Belshazzar, King of Babylon, has given a feast using precious vessels stolen from the Temple of Solomon. At the height of the banquet a mysterious hand appears and writes on the wall, portending the destruction of the city and the death of Belshazzar himself. Rembrandt shows the moment when the king turns around in terror and his guests are thrown into confusion, freezing his characters at the point of maximum drama. This theatrical approach to narrative painting is typical of much seventeenth-century Baroque painting, and has its roots in the work of Caravaggio. The same is true of the compositional device of showing the figures in half-length, pushed close to the picture plane and set against a neutral background.

Though the composition is rather derivative, particularly in the forms of the woman on the extreme right, Rembrandt demonstrates a stunning virtuosity in the range of different painting techniques, and one can see very clearly the stages by which he has built up the composition. He has begun with a brown underlayer, providing a unifying tone to the finished work, visible in the shadows beneath the king's outspread arm and the base color of the tablecloth. He then mapped out the general areas of his forms in cool, "dead" colors — tempera may have been used for these because of its quick-drying qualities. He seems in general to have dispensed with preparatory drawings (very few exist) and to have developed his forms directly in paint as he went along. In the greenish gray coloring of the shadowy flute player to the rear of the lefthand group, one can see the base color from which he fleshed out the skin tones in the other figures. The same green is visible beneath the flesh tints of the bearded man, and have also been used to define the broad outlines of the tablecloth. The dark brown underpainting is visible beneath the red of the woman's gown on the far right. Here one can see Rembrandt's skillful manner of mapping out the general form by "kissing" the dark undercoat with a thin layer of red and then building up a sense of volume by subsequent strokes of the same color, applied thickly enough to be only partially modified by the darker paint beneath. Additional thick dashes of the same red are applied last to suggest those lightest parts where light catches the folds of the material.

It is in the handling of Belshazzar's richly jeweled gown, however, that the virtuosity of handling is most obviously apparent. The effect of the encrustation of gold embroidery and precious stones is rendered in thick swathes of yellow impasto that have been literally modeled in relief with a pointed brush and then partly carved away with a sharp instrument. This method of descriptive modeling is in sharp constrast to the broad suggestion of form that can be seen in passages such as the small plate at the edge of the table on the left, which has been lightly suggested in a couple of loose sweeps of light gray against the original brown underpaint. Such variety of handling shows the young Rembrandt's complete mastery of his medium.

In this, the most theatrical of Rembrandt's paintings discussed here, one can follow very clearly the stages by which the artist has built up his composition. Few other works contain such a wide range of brushwork: from the modeling of the jeweled clasp in thick wet impasto to the rich glazing technique in the far lefthand figure or the broad and confident directional brushwork seen in the folds of the red sleeve.

1

2

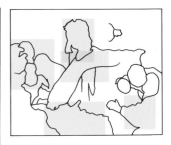

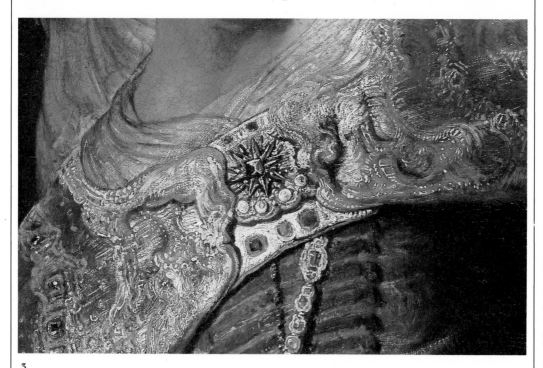

3

4

1 The ghostly face of the musician behind the main group shows the first stage of underpainting in dull green from which all the other figures have emerged.

2 The forms of the red sleeve have been achieved by using the same red but in differing degrees of thickness against the brown underpainting. The freely applied squiggles and loops of the drapery suggest the arm's implicit movement.

3 The decoration of the cloak and the jeweled clasp was achieved with two brushes: one thick and rounded, the other fine and pointed. The first was used to create broad grooves, perhaps also using the handle of the brush to create three-dimensional ridges. Touches of wet white were then applied with the pointed brush, with yellow to provide the highlights.

4 The tablecloth is painted in dull green over the brown underpaint, the pattern picked out in thin strokes of white. The plates are conceived with great economy, in rough, sweeping strokes of white or yellow which catch in the grooves of the underpainting, suggesting reflected highlights. The still life of grapes has been very simply drawn in a series of muddy half-tones, set off by touches of white highlight.

5 The head of Belshazzar has been firmly modeled in flesh tones, the highlights and half-shadows painted upon a tan middle ground, most obvious in the nose. Parts of the turban have been very thinly painted and have become transparent with age.

5

SELF-PORTRAIT

Signed and dated 1640
39⅜×31½in/100×80cm
Oil on canvas
National Gallery, London

Rembrandt here has depicted himself as the successful painter, dressed expensively and with an expression of calm assurance. The Baroque rhythms and exuberant outward show which had governed his work throughout the previous decade have been replaced by a sense of "gravitas," echoed in the stable triangular form and the stressed horizontals of cap and sill as well as by the alert but reserved expression. The idea of including the *trompe l'oeil* device of the parapet is a rather artificial convention that had been widely used in Renaissance art, and in fact Rembrandt based his composition on Titian's *Portrait of a Man with Blue Sleeve* (see opposite), widely believed at the time to represent Ludovico Ariosto, the famous Italian poet. At the time this painting was in the collection of Alphonso Lopez, a rich Spanish diamond dealer who also dealt in and collected works of art. He possessed an early Rembrandt, and from extant letters it is clear that they were acquainted with each other. Rembrandt saw in this work and in other Renaissance paintings a restraint and dignity which he found increasingly congenial to the tenor of his own art, but the borrowing from Titian may have a deeper significance as well. It has been suggested that in following Titian so obviously, Rembrandt was consciously comparing himself, the painter, with Ariosto, the poet, and thus claiming a status for painting equal to that of poetry, in the spirit of a theory of the arts that goes back to the Renaissance.

Perhaps taking his lead from Titian, the portrait is much more thinly painted than in the previous works examined here, and he has paid minute attention to descriptive details. The lighting is strong but quite diffuse, the intensity of the strongest lights on cheek, chest and hand softened by a subtle range of half-tones and transparent shadows. The background is relatively light, made up of delicately scumbled greenish yellow and light brown strokes laid over a darker brown underlayer, very obvious by the left cheek and sleeve. This helps to create a greater impression of space between the figure and the background. A sense of shimmering, diffused light is created by the interplay of the thin top layer and the darker tone beneath. The face is very delicately painted, with soft fluid colors built up from a greenish gray base in a series of slightly varying flesh tones blended delicately and almost imperceptibly together. Rembrandt has used at least three different kinds of red — a dullish pink for the cheeks, a more orange-red for the nose and a deeper crimson for the mouth. The passages around the eyes and mouth are made up of extraordinarily delicate touches, applied with a very thin pointed brush on a thin underlayer of wet paint. This delicate pattern of thin blended colors not only builds up the forms of the face, but describes the texture, the color and the exact tonal quality dictated by the fall of light.

The sleeve is more broadly painted in a sequence of browns and blacks, the darkest areas glazed over with additional layers of translucent black and the middle tones and highlights picked out in thicker passages of reddish browns and yellows.

Of all Rembrandt's self-portraits, this is perhaps his most overtly public statement, in its virtuosity of handling, its high degree of finish, and its assured, challenging, bearing.

Comparison with Titian's *Man with Blue Sleeve* shows the artist's obvious debt to the Venetian master in terms of pose, the use of the parapet, and the prominence of the sleeve. Yet Rembrandt has made many modifications. The lighting is less dramatically focused and more diffuse than in the Titian, the pose is less in profile, and the sleeve has lost the rhetorical assertiveness of the earlier picture.

TITIAN
Man With Blue Sleeve
c 1512 National Gallery, London

Titian's youthful masterpiece transformed an older tradition of portraiture and established a new canon. Much greater prominence was given to the torso, and here its elegant *contrapposto* helps to convey the sitter's assured and confident personality. The splendid sleeve, the dramatic lighting and the proud assertive stare combine to make this work one of the epoch-making images in the history of portraiture.

1

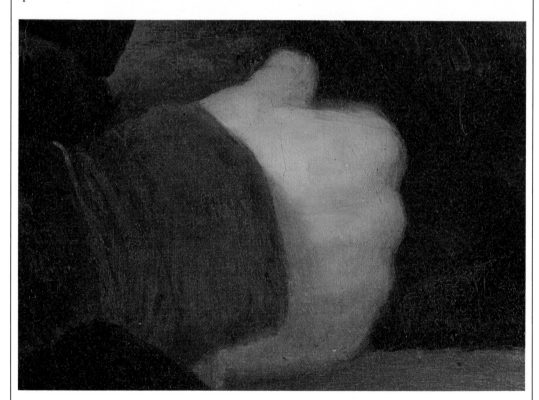

2

1 The sleeve is painted in a sequence of broadly applied glazes over a general area of brown, the darkest areas rendered in translucent black. The details of the running seams are picked out in lighter, muddy browns and touches of thick yellow impasto.

2 The brightly lit hand is handled in a very broad manner, the forms of the fist only very roughly drawn, and the lightest parts applied in a thick layer of pre-mixed flesh tones over the darker brown of the shadowed area.

3 *Actual size detail* The flesh tones of the face are built up in a series of glazes of the utmost subtlety, each blending all but imperceptibly into the wet layer beneath in a manner that calls for extreme precision of handling. The pouches and lines around the eyes — the part of the face that perhaps reveals most about the artist's character, creating a sense of vulnerability, even anxiety, around the alert stare — are minutely drawn. Very thin brown paint has been used, merging into the wet, lighter skin tone beneath so that they lose their quality as "lines," and assume the character of the shadowed declivities and puckers of the skin.

3 *Actual size detail*

THE NIGHT WATCH

Signed and dated 1642
141¼ × 172½ in / 359 × 438 cm
Oil on canvas
Rijksmuseum, Amsterdam

This is perhaps Rembrandt's most celebrated work, as famous among his contemporaries as it is today. Its name is in fact a mistitling, as after cleaning it was found to be a day scene, and it shows the Militia Company of Arquebusiers under the command of Captain Frans Banning Cocq and his lieutenant, Willem van Ruytenburch, preparing to march out. Each city in Holland had a number of militia companies, originally formed for defense in the war against Spain. By 1640, however, the threat to peace had largely evaporated and the companies had grown into societies of high-ranking citizens, somewhat resembling gentleman's clubs. This painting was commisioned to hang in the newly built wing of the company headquarters, along with seven other canvases of militia group portraits by other artists. But as Rembrandt's pupil Samuel van Hoogstraten wrote in a biography of his master, such was the picture's daring and originality of conception that "in comparison, according to some, all the other pieces there look like packs of playing cards."

The work represents the apogee of Rembrandt's treatment of the group portrait, for he has completely subordinated the demands of portraiture to those of large-scale narrative painting with unprecedented originality. (Each sitter paid a sum commensurate with his prominence within the painting.) The Captain is ordering his lieutenant to give the signal of departure, and the other members of the company adopt appropriate gestures in readiness, one loading a musket, another raising the standard, the drummer beating a roll on his drum and so on. The names of eighteen members of the company depicted are inscribed on the stone cartouche to the right of the portal, and the scene has been fleshed out with a number of peripheral figures, including dogs and children (Rembrandt's own features can be glimpsed to the immediate right of the standard-bearer's shoulder). Onto this complex arrangement of figures Rembrandt has imposed a lively pattern of chiaroscuro combined with a palette of rich color, both of which serve to emphasize the chief protagonists. The dominant combination of deep red, lemon yellow and black that make up the two central characters is repeated and echoed in touches throughout the whole composition, most notably in the red uniform of the musketeer and the bright yellow of the little girl to the right of the central group. Her prominence is explained by the claws of the chicken at her belt – claws were the symbol of the company — and this points up the fact that the scene is symbolic rather than a faithful representation of an actual event.

No other work shows quite such rich and varied handling of the brush: in the thin and schematic painting of the background architecture; in the rapid sequence of glazes that make up the standard-bearer's sash; in the minutely drawn "high-relief" modeling of the trimmings of the lieutenant's tunic; and finally, in the broad suggestion of velvet folds in the righthand musketeer's costume, done by free sweeps and clotted question-marks of thick red paint. Despite the fact that the work was cut down at the top and sides in the eighteenth century, it remains, in its ingenuity of composition and variety of technique, one of Rembrandt's most successful works.

This is one of Rembrandt's largest extant works, and in few other paintings has he displayed such a wide range of brushwork. It acts as both a group portrait and as a narrative composition, and technique has been used in the service of both traditions.

Passages of highly detailed descriptive painting, combined with bright lighting, accentuate certain key figures and differentiate them from the mass, while other subsidiary figures — some are not actual portraits — are more generally treated.

1

1 The handling of paint on the red-clothed figure presents a great contrast with that of the girl (see opposite); it is far less detailed and more loosely handled. The dark underlayer is traceable in the brown tinge of the shadows, and the colors have been worked up in a broad, thin red overlay that allows the brown to show through. Onto this were superimposed the bright reds and darks of the folds, the brushstrokes being particularly evident in the highlights beneath the right arm.

2 The strange, symbolic motif of a dead chicken hung from the waist of the small girl has been given a deliberate prominence by the use of bright colors that form a striking contrast with the darker tones of the surrounding figures, particularly the silhouette of the musket in front. The shimmering brightness of both the dress and the feathers of the chicken has been achieved by the application of closely painted lemon yellow against a darker ground layer, highlighted with thick lead-white impasto. The suggestion of rich embroidery on the collar has been achieved by a great variety of brushstrokes, from small descriptive dashes along the hem to thin glazes of blue and passages of thick white impasto for the brightest parts.

2

3

4

3 The head, or part of a face, glimpsed on the far left above the shoulder of the man in armor is traditionally supposed to be a self-portrait, although such is its obscurity that it is impossible to be certain. Given the nature of the commission — a large-scale figurative scene — it is possible that Rembrandt was aware of and was following a well-established self-portrait tradition that went back to the Italian Renaissance.

4 The painting was cut down at the sides at some point after its execution and the figure of the drummer and the man immediately above him have been seriously curtailed. The apparent lack of finish to the face of the drummer, as compared with the treatment of the other faces, is probably due to damaged paint surface rather than any deliberate device of the artist. His sleeve and drum are rendered with painstaking care.

5 The extremely high degree of finish of the passages of embroidery and in the ceremonial spear constitute the most detailed parts of the whole painting. In the treatment of the clasps securing the jacket there is a literal description of forms modeled in high relief that is comparable to the treatment of details in the earlier *Tobit and Anna* (see page 17). The gold- and pearl-embroidered border and leggings have been executed over a broadly painted yellow ground in small loops and dashes of brown paint, with occasional stronger accents of the same color in the areas of shadow. These have been overlaid with touches of tawny yellow and tiny points of white impasto.

5

THE ADORATION OF THE SHEPHERDS

Signed and dated 1646
25³⁄₄×21³⁄₄in/65.5×55cm
Oil on canvas
National Gallery, London

In this work one can see the sharp change in style that had become apparent in Rembrandt's work by the mid-1640s. The canvas is quite small, and the mood evoked is one of quiet and restraint. The gestures of the assembled figures are entirely natural, with none of the rhetoric of *The Night Watch* or *Belshazzar's Feast*, and they have clearly been studied carefully from life. Rembrandt approaches the mystery of the Nativity from a wholly human standpoint; indeed the only symbolic element that might suggest supernatural significance is the extraordinary light that seems to emanate from the Christchild, bathing the onlookers in a mysterious glow. This symbolic function of light is accompanied by a new breadth of technique. Rembrandt applies the colors in flat, succinct brushstrokes which now barely serve to model form or indicate texture. The Virgin's face, arm and torso, for example, are made up from a small number of dabs of unmodulated color, which only assume the suggestion of form when viewed from a distance. A single brushstroke of thick, creamy black suggests the forms of the ox's neck, the ridges of paint on either side of it reflecting light and thus giving an actual impression of three-dimensional form. The kneeling shepherd immediately in front of the Christchild has been created by a few strokes in black against the darker brown background which describe with the utmost economy his attitude of deep humility. This painting style is directly related to his manner of drawing at this time in which all extraneous details are sacrificed to the task of catching in its most concentrated form that attitude of a figure which best reveals its inner state. By suggesting form rather than carefully describing it Rembrandt bypasses the surface distractions of the external world and concentrates on the expression of pure feeling. The result is an image of extraordinary emotional power.

This is heightened by the lighting, which creates a warm, hazy, atmospheric effect which muffles features and mingles forms and shadows. The highlights that describe the Christchild contrast with the thinner treatment of the light shed by the lantern, falling in muted pools on the ground in the lower righthand side. This effect is created by a loose wet-into-wet technique in which touches of lighter color are painted onto a wet, dark brown undercoat, so that at times the lighter color is modified by mixing with the brown. The uneven, mottled effect made in this way provides a rich surface texture that, together with the range of carefully calculated half-tones and reflections, creates an atmosphere of hushed mystery in which the figures play out their solemn roles.

This is one of several small-scale Biblical works of the 1640s in which the figures are treated in the tradition of contemporary Dutch *genre* painting. It may possibly reflect the beliefs of the Mennonites, a Protestant sect which placed great importance on the Biblical injunction to "love thy neighbor" and with which Rembrandt is known to have been closely associated. This could have had some bearing on the way Rembrandt expressed divine events in everyday, down-to-earth terms, easily accessible to his contemporaries, and with an emphasis on individual humility and quiet devotion.

1 The warm atmosphere of the central group is extended even to the rafters in the outermost part of the composition, where the reflected lights are made up of touches of red and orange-yellow set against the deep brown of the shadows. Once again the broad handling is accompanied by a complex tonal range.

2 The details of boy and dog have been picked out over a brown underlayer of small, thin touches of paint. Tiny dabs of red indicate the local color of the tunic; touches of deeper brown and black articulate folds and shadows; the outlines of the dog have been picked out very simply in white highlight and touches of black against the dark ground.

3 The ox has been sketched in with great economy in a sequence of thin, warm browns; the collarbone, ears and front part of the head roughly outlined in black, while the throat and mouth have been picked out in lighter brown, palely reflecting the light of the central group. A single creamy brushstroke, applied so as to leave ridges on either side, suggests in almost literal three-dimensional form the shape of the neck.

4 *Actual size detail* The simplicity and economy of Rembrandt's brushwork is very clearly shown in this detail, in which expressions are caught with the smallest touches of paint. The paint is very thin here, with the folds of drapery, half-tones and local colors indicated by small, free touches of tinted varnish over a medium-dark ground. The areas of thickest color are reserved for the most strongly lit parts, for instance the Christchild's swaddling clothes and the figure of the Virgin. The warm, hazy *sfumato* effect is achieved by an almost imperceptible mingling of yellows and browns of varying tone that charges the atmosphere and merges the figures and surrounding space.

Young Woman Bathing

Signed and dated 1655
24³⁄₈×18¹⁄₂in/62×47cm
Oil on canvas
National Gallery, London

This work vividly demonstrates Rembrandt's growing ability to combine rich color harmonies with a complex chiaroscuro system and an astonishingly broad and sensual handling of paint. In certain passages, the brushstrokes have become almost independent of the forms they describe. The small scale and spontaneous quality of the painting suggests an oil sketch, although Rembrandt has chosen to sign and date it.

Any precise indication of the work's subject has been left unclear, although the richly embroidered garments on the river bank perhaps suggest the Old Testament subject of "Susannah Bathing." It shows a rather stockily built woman, traditionally thought to be Hendrickje Stoffels, carefully raising her undershirt as she wades into the water, apparently completely wrapped in thought. Her beauty lies in the unconscious way in which she unwittingly reveals her upper thighs, a potentially erotic gesture which is emptied of any lascivious content by its very naturalness. Rembrandt's conception of beauty lies, not so much in the idea of inherent beauty of form, but in the revelation, often in a private moment, of an unstudied attitude of grace which captures the inner, private character.

The variety of brushwork is dazzling. The outline of the figure has been roughly mapped out in dark brown strokes, which convey a marvelous sense of volume and of underlying bone structure, as for example in the definition of the right arm and hand. The flesh tones of the face and legs have been strongly modeled with fluidly applied directional brushstrokes of varying tinges of flesh color, blended wet-into-wet and applied so as to follow the shape of the forms they describe. These contrast vividly with the treatment of the shirt, which is made up of loose strokes of beige, light blue and yellow, laid beneath a thrilling sequence of thick impasto strokes of creamy white, smeared with extraordinary freedom with the brush and palette knife, and gouged in places with the brush handle, leaving ridges in high relief. These describe almost literally the three-dimensional form in the folds of the cloth.

The right forearm is articulated by a single flat brushstroke extending from elbow to wrist, which succeeds in conveying volume when viewed from a distance. The left shoulder and arm have been treated in a very abstract manner, the lines of the initial rapid sketch clearly visible, the sleeve of the shirt barely glazed over the light brown underpaint, and the arm composed merely of flat lozenges of highlights and darks. The background and righthand side of the painting have been thrown into deep shadow by a varnish of dark glazes that spills over onto the shoulder and partly obscures the face. Once again the shadows establish the mood of the work and deepen the sense of the young woman's rapt self-absorption. The same shadows seep into the colored reflections in the water, which are magically suggested by thin, fluid glazes of deep red, browns and golden yellows over a light beige underlayer, the gentle ripples picked out in touches of white impasto. In few other works does Rembrandt so skillfully interweave lights and darks with so suggestive and allusive a touch.

The breadth of handling, richness of color and complex range of chiaroscuro in this small-scale, intimate work are the hallmarks of Rembrandt's style in the 1650s. The breathtaking variety of technique shows his complete mastery of the "suggestive" brushstroke. The broad, creamy strokes of the undershirt, the rounded, directional modeling of the legs, the flat, translucent glazes of the reflections of the pool and the abstract hatching of the left arm all precisely denote the quality of the elements they describe, and combine harmoniously.

1

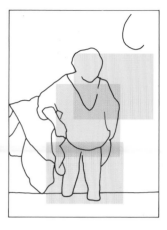

1 Divorced from its context the left arm appears almost abstract in its lack of descriptive modeling. A rough black outline defines the upper arm, and a thin brown glaze, sketchily applied, indicates the sleeve of the shirt in semi-shadow, set off by an errant touch of white at the edge. The forearm has been articulated solely by contrasting patches of white and dark brown paint. The background is equally undefined and for the most part left in rich brown shadow. The forms of a tree on the river bank have been roughly picked out in a very thin, tawny reddish-brown.

2 The firm, directional modeling of the legs and knees conveys the impression of heavy, dimpled flesh, and contrasts with the thin, diaphanous treatment of the water. Threads of thick, dry white paint mark the point where the legs break the surface of the water.

3 *Actual size detail* The rough outlining in brown is evident at the hem of the undershirt, and in the definition of the arm, wrist and knuckled hand. The ridged and smeared three-dimensional quality of the thick, white impasto strokes of the folds of the cloth is clearly shown above a beige ground. This contrasts with the more modeled areas of flesh, where the individual strokes are smaller and merge together more. The shadows of the neck and shoulders have been deepened with additional glazes of very dark brown.

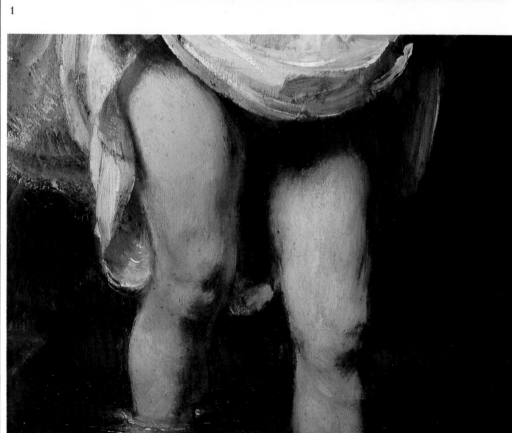

2

3 *Actual size detail*

THE DENIAL OF ST PETER

Signed and dated 1660
60½×66½/154×169cm
Oil on canvas
Rikjsmuseum, Amsterdam

Painted in the last decade of Rembrandt's life, this is one of his last great religious paintings, and represents the culmination of a lifetime's exploration of Biblical narrative. Rembrandt is the supreme interpreter of the Bible, and he devoted a very substantial part of his total output to the genre, even though he lived in a predominantly Calvinist society that by and large did little to encourage religious imagery. The fact that very few of his religious works were either commissioned by churches or were intended to hang in them says much about his independence as an artist and his compulsion to paint only what preoccupied him, often in the face of fashionable and commercial indifference. In the 1630s he had been fascinated by scenes of extravagance and drama; in the 1640s a preference for gentler, more domestic scenes prevailed; in the later 1650s and 1660s he dwelt on more somber themes of human dilemma and fallibility. In this painting the whole drama is concentrated on the figure of the saint, whose face powerfully expresses a range of conflicting emotions — fear, shame, even despair — when confronted by the fierce questioners on the lefthand side. On the upper right, the figure of Christ can dimly be discerned, turning his back at the moment of his chief apostle's fall from faith.

The composition and handling are extremely simplified, and almost give the impression of being unfinished. Rembrandt has concentrated his whole effort on the face of St Peter himself with every other element treated in as sketchy a manner as possible. As in a number of his later works, there is a tendency to concentrate on the expression of a single emotion or reaction almost at the expense of the narrative that produced it, and here it is obvious that his real interest lies in St Peter's inner turmoil rather than in the more superficial, outward drama of the confrontation with his accusers.

The whole work is very loosely painted, and there is no attempt at precise descriptive modeling. This gives an impression of flatness to various parts of the painting, particularly on the lower lefthand side. The figure on the far left is articulated solely by means of extremely broad strokes of black and orange-red brushed onto the brown underpaint. The soldier in armor is scarcely better finished; he is sketched in in a manner that in earlier works would have constituted the underpainting. His forehead and nose are no more than rough wedges of pinkish-red paint, quite formlessly applied. The helmet in the lower foreground has been conceived purely in terms of reflected lights, thinly painted over the dark undercoat, and throughout the painting there are passages of equally broadly applied brushstrokes, falling in open juxtaposition to each other and only merging in the eye when seen from some distance. Even the face of St Peter, half-captured in the light of the flickering taper, is made up of relatively simplified brushstrokes. The shadows that course around the furrows of his face wonderfully convey his troubled mood.

This large-scale work is remarkable for its extremely free handling and sketch-like manner and represents the increasing looseness of technique of Rembrandt's last years. It has to be seen from a considerable distance before the brushstrokes and clotted patches of color assume recognizable forms. Compositionally Rembrandt has returned to the large-scale, half-length figures and the dramatic flickering light of a concealed taper that he learned from the "Caravaggesque" painters of the Utrecht school early in his career, but here the drama is less theatrical and is concentrated instead on St Peter's inner turmoil.

1

2

1 The simplicity, even roughness, of the paint application, is particularly marked in the maidservant's right hand, where the forefinger has been made up from a thick wedge of pink. The heads to her left are even more cursorily described in the same dull pink highlights that bring out the pugnacious jaw and protruding lower lip set against the deep brown and black of the main silhouette. Further touches of muted pink just hint at the metallic glint of the helmet.

2 The figure of Christ amid his captors, turning back to witness his betrayal at the hands of his chief disciple, forms the secondary narrative focus, and is thus appropriately muted. The figures only emerge dimly from the dark underpainting, created by strokes of deep brown and black, and highlighted by touches of a subdued reddish-brown.

3 *Actual size detail* The furrowed brow and shadowed face of St Peter have been articulated by a patchwork of varied local flesh tones, with additional light and dark accents that overlap each other and remain largely unblended.

3 *Actual size detail*

MARGARETHA DE GEER

Signed and dated 1661
29¾×25¼in/75.5×64cm
Oil on canvas
National Gallery, London

Margaretha de Geer was the wife of a Dordrecht merchant, Jacob Trip, whose portrait Rembrandt also painted at about the same time. This portrait is a marvelous depiction of old age, drawn with a rare combination of sympathy and objectivity. The dramatic focus of the work is created by the vivid contrast between the brilliant white of the collar and the surrounding darkness, which has the effect of dramatically drawing attention to the head, though the impact is softened by the half-tones of the face itself. The starched brilliance of the collar also creates a telling contrast with the wrinkled and puckered skin, serving to throw emphasis on the subject's bodily frailty and thus producing an intimation of mortality. Though she looks out at the spectator, her stare is unfocused, giving the impression of private reverie which, together with the dark shadows behind, produces a contemplative, even somber mood. The extreme simplicity of the composition and the complete lack of any recognizable environment removes her from any specific social context and thus allows her "inner," private self to become the focus.

The way the face has been built is extraordinary. The roughest outlines have been sketched in, defining cheekbones and articulating the jawline. Thereafter, very small touches of modulated flesh colors, from a dull bluish gray to dull rose, have been applied in overlapping sequence, at times following the direction of the face, at times quite flatly applied. The paint-strokes are thick, so that the surface of the face is broken and uneven, giving the mottled effect of withered skin. The forms of the nose are articulated purely in variations of color — there is no line — and from a close viewpoint are rather indistinct, yet the tones precisely match the quality of the light falling on the face.

The lace collar has been painted with great delicacy. The thin ridges of lace have been picked out in minute strokes of white impasto over a diaphanous glaze of the same color modified by the darker hue beneath. In the treatment of the lower tier of the collar, the hollow parts have been "kissed" with a very dry yellowish tone, leaving the dark brown underpainting visible, and the forms of the lace have been picked out delicately on top in loose strokes of white with the brightest accents made up of tiny drops of white impasto. The result is a thrilling passage of monochrome painting, from which the exact quality of lace emerges by means of slight variations of the same color.

The somber, introspective quality of this portrait offers some explanation of Rembrandt's waning popularity as a portrait painter in his later years. Most people who commissioned a portrait required an image of themselves that emphasized their social status and gave some sense of their place in the world. Few would have desired to be the subject of such a searching exploration of their private selves or to have seen themselves portrayed as so vunerable to the effects of time and old age. Here Rembrandt has gone far beyond the usual requirements of portraiture — of displaying a good likeness and a sense of character — to produce an image containing far deeper and more universal layers of meaning.

1 The detail shows the stages by which the lace collar has been worked up from the dark underpainting. A layer of white has been broadly applied, and has been slightly modified by the dark brown beneath. Details of the lace have then been picked out in threads of dry white impasto, using a fine pointed brush.

The torso has been very simply treated so that it does not divert attention away from the face. The gown is made up of black glazes and the buttons have been picked out in touches in yellow.

2 *Actual size detail* This detail shows clearly both the variety of skin tone employed in building up the face and the delicacy and precision with which they have been applied. Each slight modulation matches exactly, not only the varitions of color and tone, but also the variations of texture and form that make up the face. The brushwork concentrates more on effects of textures and tone than on color, and even the thin strokes of pure white in the brow, on the cheeks and along the line of the nose merge with the other flesh tones so that they partake of the quality of skin as well as denoting reflected highlights.

1

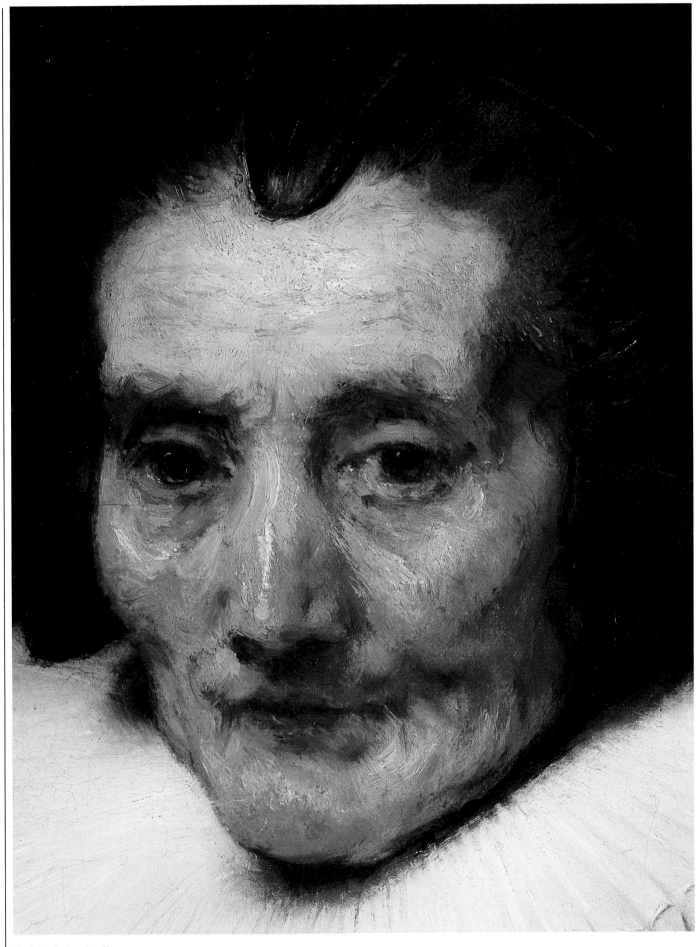

2 *Actual size detail*

SELF-PORTRAIT WITH MAULSTICK, PALETTE AND BRUSHES

c 1663

28⅜×30in/72×76cm

Oil on canvas

Iveagh Bequest, Kenwood House, London

This somber work is both a moving example of Rembrandt's late style and a revealing image of the artist in his late middle-age. In contrast to the self-portrait of 1640 (see page 29), this is an image of the artist at work, roughly dressed in simple tunic and painter's cap, holding his palette, maulstick and brushes as he surveys his canvas. While the portrayal of the artist in his studio, surrounded by the tools of his professions and often accompanied by exotic or "learned" studio props was by no means uncommon in seventeenth-century Holland, this work is exceptional in its stark, unadorned simplicity. There is no attempt to create a fashionable environment, or to make a case for the gentlemanly nature of the artist's profession. Instead it conveys a powerful sense of the rough simplicity of the painter's craft. In doing so Rembrandt has also endowed his image with a monumental grandeur equaled by few other self-portraits. This is achieved by the arrangement of the composition into stark geometrical forms of triangle and circles, as well as by the artist's imposing bulk, which takes up a large proportion of the picture surface. In addition, the searching, self-scrutinizing expression confirms the deep seriousness with which Rembrandt approaches his art.

Rembrandt painted his own features repeatedly throughout his career, sometimes in order to study different expressions and poses, sometimes dressing himself up in exotic costumes and posing as some Biblical character. There are, however, a large number of self-portraits which appear to have been made for their own sake, and which offer clues to the artist's real character. This work is one such.

It is painted with stunning breadth, and though the palette is restricted to a relatively limited range of colors, they are arranged in telling combinations and contrasts. The head is composed of a rich sequence of loose directional strokes and dabs which suggest the forms they describe, for instance the single brushstroke that follows the right side of the jaw or the tiny dabs of yellowish white that exactly describe the slight concavity of the skull to the left of the eye-socket. A marvelous interweaving of light and shadow is created by the application of dabs of differing color that also vary in tone. Thus the dull pink of the left cheek is a carefully calculated middle-tone, caught between deeper shadows, whereas the different flesh colors on the more brightly illuminated right cheek are chosen for their lighter tonal values.

The paint has been applied in thick, rich strokes of a heavily loaded brush, wet-on-wet, to provide a sensual mingling of the paint layers. The stiff hairs of the brush leave behind minute troughs and valleys that reveal the paint beneath and thus create a rich, broken surface texture that reflects actual light and conveys both an impression of three-dimensional form and the actual texture of skin. The effect of the mustache has been created by scribbling with a sharp instrument directly into the wet paint.

As in many of his mature portraits, a suggestiveness of mood is evoked by concealing the exact expression of the eyes in deep shadow so that the spectator is forced to use his own imagination to complete the expression. The fluctuation of the shadows, created by varying the degrees of dark tones, strengthens the impression of a somber inner mood. Rembrandt has brought an objectivity of approach, an intellectual honesty and a depth of insight to bear on his own features that place this painting among the greatest works of confessional autobiography of any age.

This self-portrait is of an additional, incidental interest because it shows the tools with which Rembrandt approached his craft: a rectangular palette, maulstick and a number of brushes. These last are too indistinctly drawn to be able to identify with any certainty the types of brush he used, but from the evidence of his canvases it is probable that he used stiff hog's-hair brushes with a blunt end for the broad passages, and a series of fine, pointed ones for more detailed work. The curious and unsual motif of the circles in the background of the painting has not been satisfactorily explained, but they combine with the triangular bulk of the figure to divide the picture into large, austerely simple geometric shapes, enhancing the feeling of brooding monumentality.

1

1 The impression of wild, unkempt curls of graying hair is achieved by small directional strokes of a dull ocher, applied with quite a thick brush, over which small amounts of white impasto have been dragged. The impression left by the hairs of the brush and the direction the stroke has taken are clearly visible. The large, thick, white rectangular strokes that make up the folds of the cap form a strong contrast with the dull green of the background.

2 No attempt has been made to define the hand holding the palette and brushes. The tools themselves are executed in swift strokes that lose definition when seen from close at hand. The palette has been roughly painted over the black of the artist's coat so that the latter is plainly visible beneath.

3 *Actual size detail* The breadth of handling, the density of the paint surface and the variety of colors are vividly displayed in this detail. A light, grayish-green underpainting is discernible in the middle tones of the face, onto which a range of dull reds, pinks, orange and even yellow have been worked, in overlapping, wet-on-wet layers to build form and color. A single line of black strengthens the right eyelid; another dimly defines the fold under the chin.

2

3 *Actual size detail*

THE JEWISH BRIDE

Signed and (indistinctly) dated c 1665-68
47³/₄×65½in/121.5×166.5cm
Oil on canvas
Rikjsmuseum, Amsterdam

The true subject of this work is unknown, and its title was invented in the early nineteenth century. It has been variously suggested that it represents a wedding portrait; is one of several Biblical pairs such as Esther and Ahasuerus, Isaac and Rebecca or Jacob and Rachel; or is a representation of a bridal couple in the guise of Biblical characters. This last is the most probable since it was a custom not without precedents in earlier art. Certainly the man's gesture can be seen as belonging to a tradition of portraying Jacob and Rachel that goes back to at least the fifteenth century.

However, whether it is a portrait or a Biblical scene, the real topic of this work is the expression of complete physical and spiritual union. In an immensely gentle gesture the man seems symbolically to "take possession" of the woman, whose answering touch signifies her acquiescence. The gesture serves to imply the physical nature of their union, yet the tenderness with which it is bestowed, coupled with the deep solemnity of their expressions, raises it to an almost symbolic level of all-embracing feeling that goes far beyond the merely amorous. The marked simplicity of composition, with the concentration of lighting in the upper torsos to the exclusion of any circumstantial detail, shows Rembrandt's ability to isolate and to dwell on a single emotion or psychological state. The deep shadows that envelop the couple help to place them outside time or specific location and thus to generalize the emotion conveyed.

The tender mood is expressed by both the extraordinary warmth of color and the shimmering, ethereal quality of the light, which almost seems to emanate from within the figures to create a potent visual metaphor for their state of feeling. The manner of painting is extremely free, particularly in the treatment of the clothing. The man's golden sleeve is built up from a complicated system of orange-brown and yellow glazes, with the highlights laid on in the thickest possible impasto — almost like a sculpted relief frieze — applied with a brush and a palette knife in thick, regular, rectangular strokes. As with Rembrandt's other late works this painting needs to be viewed from a considerable distance before the individual strokes merge into the form of heavily textured cloth. The working of the man's tunic is also very unconventional: a thin tawny yellow has been dragged almost randomly over a dark brown underlayer and then scoured through with a sharp instrument. Passages of the woman's jewelry, particularly the golden chain around her shoulders, are applied in heavy blobs of impasto. These, when viewed close up, seem to have been put on in a random manner, but when seen from a distance miraculously assume recognizable form. The heads have been more carefully modeled in warm tones, with the red of the woman's cheek answering the deep crimson of her dress. The background consists of rough glazes worked loosely over a dark background.

In this most moving of all Rembrandt's paintings, one sees how the ageing artist completely transcends the standard stylistic conventions of his age in a completely personal style in which representation itself is all but subsumed by the expressive power of the paint-strokes themselves.

The combination of a golden yellow and deep red against a dark brown setting occurs in numerous works of Rembrandt's maturity. It is already noticeable, for instance, in the background drapery of *Young Woman Bathing* (see page 43) and again in the central section of *The Denial of St Peter* (see page 47). Here it forms the dominant color chord of the composition and confers upon the figures a dimension of warmth. The variety of yellow and red tones based around this central combination produces a work of the greatest coloristic complexity.

1

1 This detail reveals the great variety of brushwork from fairly generalized areas such as the red of the dress, where the paint has been roughly applied in coarse streaks, and the hands, painted in a variety of flesh tones, to other areas of detailed, descriptive paintwork, such as the jeweled and pearl-laden bracelet on the left wrist. Here the highlights have been picked out in measured droplets of impasto.

2 The sleeve is built up by means of thick lozenges of paint of varying tones of yellow and brown, applied in part with a palette knife, and overlaid with white impasto in the lightest areas. The paint is so thickly applied in places that some of the highlights actually stand out in three dimensions so that light is trapped in and reflected by the crevices within the paint surface. It is only from a distance that the texture of soft, golden fabric is achieved.

3 *Actual size detail* The detail shows the relatively high degree of finish that has gone into the modeling of the head. It is worked up from a dark underpainting, most clearly visible in the shadowed right side of the face. The range of colors is surprisingly large: from a dull blue and modified violet in the jaw to a whole variety of reds. These modulate from the full crimson of the lips to a series of reddish-browns leading in to the lighter flesh tones in the highlights.

2

3 *Actual size detail*

INDEX

PHOTOGRAPHIC CREDITS

The photographs in this book were provided by the following:
Bridgeman Art Library 10; British Museum, London 12 top; Iveagh
Bequest, Kenwood House, London 55-57; Kunstammlungen,
Dresden 12 bottom; National Gallery, London 6, 7, 8, 9, 25-27, 29-
31, 39-41, 43-45, 51-53; Rijksmuseum, Amsterdam 17-19, 21-23,
33-37, 47-49, 59-61; Visual Arts Library, London 13 top and bottom.